spot

SPORTS

GYMNASTICS

by Mari Schuh

AMICUS | AMICUS INK

beam

chalk

Look for these words and pictures as you read.

mat

vault

The gymnasts are ready.

The meet starts.

It will last two hours.

The meet has many events.
Let's watch!

chalk

Do you see the chalk?

It keeps hands dry.

All set!

Do you see the vault?
A gymnast runs. She jumps.
Then she twists. Good job!

vault

Do you see the beam?
It is long. A gymnast
jumps. Then she turns.
Well done!

beam

Do you see the mat?
It is thick.
It is made of foam.

mat

A gymnast flips two times and lands. She runs and leaps again. Way to go!

Do you see the beam? It is long. A gymnast jumps. Then she turns. Well done!
beam

beam

chalk
Do you see the chalk? It keeps hands dry. All set!

chalk

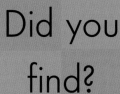

Did you find?

mat

vault

Do you see the mat? It is thick. It is made of foam.
mat

Do you see the vault? A gymnast runs. She jumps. Then she twists. Good job!
vault

Spot is published by Amicus and Amicus Ink
P.O. Box 1329, Mankato, MN 56002
www.amicuspublishing.us

Library of Congress Cataloging-in-Publication Data
Names: Schuh, Mari C., 1975- author.
Title: Gymnastics / by Mari Schuh.
Description: Mankato, Minnesota : Amicus, 2018. | Series: Spot.
  Sports | Audience: K to Grade 3.
Identifiers: LCCN 2016057197 (print) | LCCN 2016058335
  (ebook) | ISBN 9781681510873 (library binding) | ISBN
  9781681522067 (pbk.) | ISBN 9781681511771 (ebook)
Subjects: LCSH: Gymnastics--Juvenile literature. | Picture
puzzles--Juvenile literature.
Classification: LCC GV461.3 .S38 2018 (print) | LCC GV461.3
(ebook) | DDC 796.44--dc23
LC record available at https://lccn.loc.gov/2016057197

Printed in China

HC 10 9 8 7 6 5 4 3 2 1
PB 10 9 8 7 6 5 4 3 2 1

Rebecca Glaser, editor
Deb Miner, series designer
Aubrey Harper, book designer
Holly Young, photo researcher

Photos by: AP Photo/Charlie
Riedel, 14–15; iStock, cover, 1,
16; Getty Images/David Ramos,
8–9, Corbis/Tim Clayton, 10–11,
AFP/Antonin Thuillier, 12–13;
Newscom/EPA/How Hwee
Young, 3, Reuters/Sergio Moraes,
4–5, MCT/David Eulitt, 6–7

GYMNASTICS